A
Sporting
Chance

A Sporting Chance

SPORTS
—— and ——
GENDER

ANDY STEINER

Lerner Publications Company ▪ Minneapolis

To John

Library of Congress Cataloging-in-Publication Data

Steiner, Andy.
    A sporting chance : sports and gender / Andy Steiner.
      p. cm.
    Includes bibliographical references and index.
    ISBN 0–8225–3300–6 :
    1. Sports for women—United States—Juvenile literature. 2. Sex discrimination in sports—United States—Juvenile literature. 3. Women athletes—United States—Juvenile literature. [1. Sports for women. 2. Sex discrimination in sports. 3. Athletes.]
    I. Title.
GV709. 18.U6S84 1994
796'.0194—dc20   94–47584

Manufactured in the United States of America

1 2 3 4 5 6 – JR – 00 99 98 97 96 95

CONTENTS

CHAPTER ONE

GETTING IN THE GAME

■

The puck shoots across the ice faster than a speeding car. The goalie, protected by a helmet, face mask, and layers of thick gear, is ready. The opposing team races closer, skates shave ice, bodies thud together, and sticks duel as the puck zooms toward the goal.

The goalie glimpses the tangle of players thundering toward the goal, but focuses steadily on the puck as it streaks along. An opposing player takes a final, deadly whack. With every ounce of strength, the goalie moves to block the puck, stopping it dead with her strong, padded body.

If you are a hockey fan, this scene may be familiar. It has one twist: The goalie is a girl. Hockey is just one of many popular sports played mainly by men and boys. For years, American girls weren't allowed to play hockey on school or community teams because coaches and officials said the game was too dangerous. It was OK for boys to get cuts and bruises, but it wasn't OK for girls.

But the rules have changed. Since 1972, United States law has protected a girl's right to play any sport she chooses. The opportunities, resources, and support for

girls and women to participate in athletics are greater than at any other time in American history. Still, the playing field is not level. Sports aren't immune to society's sexist, racist, and elitist elements. Sometimes, girls who compete in "boy" sports face teasing and criticism, as do boys who play "girl" sports. Making sports opportunities available to girls has sometimes meant fewer sports opportunities for boys. Competing with and against boys has helped some girls improve their athletic abilities, but it has driven some girls and boys out of the game.

"I loved playing hockey, even when I was young," said Kelley Owen, a member of the U.S. women's hockey team. "To a certain point, playing with the boys wasn't a big deal, but so much depended on how good I was. There was always the extra challenge of being a girl and having to prove myself. I had to be the best."

Why are some sports for boys and not for girls? What makes a boy a better football player, a stronger wrestler, a superior catcher? Why shouldn't girls play, too? And what makes football or basketball a more important, more newsworthy, or more exciting sport than volleyball, field hockey, or softball?

Girls were once limited to only a few sports at most public schools. And the sports that were offered were often scaled back. For example, girls' basketball was different than boys'—no cross-court passing, and much less running. But pioneers, such as Billie Jean King and Wilma Rudolph, helped break down barriers in sports for young women. These trailblazers fought against discrimination and inspired others to follow in their footsteps. Because of their efforts, people learned that women could play sports and play them just as hard as men.

The federal government passed a law in 1972 called the Educational Amendment Act. One part of that law, Title IX, said federal money couldn't be given to public school programs that discriminated against girls. The law said schools must provide equal opportunities for boy and girl athletes. In order to continue to receive money from the federal government, most schools created teams just for girls. Only 294,000 girls participated in high school athletics in 1970-71, before the law was passed. By 1988-89 that number had risen to 1,841,252.[1]

Sports experts have learned that athletic activity is an important part of a healthy, successful lifestyle. "One of the biggest advantages of participating in sports is the increase in self-esteem that girls experience," said Judy Mahle Lutter, president of Melpomene Institute. "Sports help girls feel

Judy Mahle Lutter of the Melpomene Institute

better about their bodies, feel better about themselves."

In 1992, researchers at Melpomene Institute, a women's health and fitness research center, interviewed 76 girls between the ages of 9 and 12. They asked the girls to tell them how participating in sports made them feel about themselves, and how other people's attitudes about girls and sports affected their behavior. Girls who felt most confident about themselves and their abilities were more likely to spend more time per week participating in physical activity or sports than girls with lower levels of self-esteem.[2]

In 1991, the Athletic Footwear Association and the Youth Sports Institute of Michigan asked 10,000 young people between the ages of 10 and 18 to list the potential benefits of physical activity. The advantages cited most often were: emotional stability, improved self-confidence, enhanced assertiveness, independence, and better self-control. Harvard University researcher Carol Gilligan studied hundreds of girls. She discovered that involvement in physical activities can help girls grow up to be secure, confident women.

More and more women are earning sports scholarships to colleges and universities, and professional women athletes are featured more prominently in the news media. Professional women athletes, however, still make less money in salaries, prizes and commercial endorsements than male athletes do. Men's college basketball games are sold out, while women's teams often play in nearly empty gymnasiums. And not many girls play hockey—yet.

ONCE UPON A TIME

You may already know about the first Olympics. Held in ancient Greece, the Olympics were an opportunity for the best athletes to compete against one another in games of skill and strength. Running, archery, and riding events were among the sports contested. Winning an Olympic medal was a great honor, and athletes who participated were considered national heroes.

You may know all this, but did you know that women were not permitted to participate in the first Olympics? Did you know that women were forbidden under threat of execution to even watch the games? When you examine the history of sports, you discover that women and girls were often excluded—and not just in ancient times. In fact, women weren't officially allowed to participate in the modern-day Olympics until 1908.

The reasons women were once forbidden or discouraged from participating in sports were many. Women and girls were once considered the "weaker sex." Experts and physicians of both genders said it wasn't healthy for women to exercise strenuously because their bodies weren't as strong as men's. In 1933 the president of the American Physical Education Association said: "External stimuli such as cheering audiences, bands, etc., cause a great response in girls

Female athletes once were encumbered by long, bulky skirts and the requirement that they act "like ladies" at all times.

and are apt to upset the endocrine balance. Under emotional stress, a girl may easily overdo."[3]

Some people said sports were unladylike, and girls who liked sports were called tomboys. "Our gym teachers told us not to run too fast or we'd hurt ourselves," said one woman who attended high school in the 1960s. "She said we should try not to sweat."

Now, events dominated by women, such as gymnastics, figure skating, and volleyball, are some of the most popular Olympic sports. TV viewers in record numbers tune in to see strong female athletes like Bonnie Blair and Shannon Miller go for the gold.

ONE SMALL STEP

The Boston Marathon is America's most famous foot race. Professional and amateur athletes from all over the world dream of joining the crowd at the starting line, and many do. The race attracts thousands of runners each year.

When the Boston Marathon was founded, women weren't allowed to participate. It was believed that women couldn't endure long-distance running. (A marathon is 26.2 miles.) No woman could run the entire route, officials believed. It was too dangerous to even consider.

But some women wanted to run. In 1966, Roberta Gibb Bingay was sure she could run the entire distance. She was a fine athlete, and she had been running on her own for years. When officials told her she couldn't enter, she joined the marathon in secret, jumping out of the forsythia bushes along the sidelines when the starting gun sounded. She finished in the middle of the pack after 3 hours and 20 minutes. The next day, a headline in the *Boston Record American* read: "Bride Beats 22 Men in Marathon."

Another woman, Kathrine Switzer, followed in Roberta's footsteps. She entered the marathon in 1967, giving her name as K. Switzer. Race registration officials assumed she was a man, so she was allowed to enter. On race day, a Boston Marathon official, Bill Cloney, spotted Kathrine in the crowd of runners. He and other officials tried to push her out of the race, but other runners blocked them. She ran the rest of the way and finished, but her time was not recorded. Five years later, in 1972, women were finally allowed to compete in this race.[4]

When Boston Marathon official Jock Semple (in street clothes) tried to prevent Kathrine Switzer (No. 261) from running in the 1967 race, male runners helped her elude him.

That same year, 12 women staged a sit-down strike on the starting line of the New York Marathon. They were protesting a rule that required women to start 10 minutes before the men's race began. After sitting on the starting line for 10 minutes, they got up and ran with the men. Later, the rules were changed. Since 1972, male and female runners have started at the same time.[5]

Women and girls benefit from these efforts in obvious ways, but men and boys benefit, too. Don Sabo, a sports sociologist from D'Youville College in New York, says men have a lot to learn from women athletes. Playing side-by-side with women, he says, may help a man to "allow himself to cooperate rather than compete, to feel vulnerable rather than powerful. These are all dimensions of the human experience of sport."[6]

Boys and men might also benefit from an environment in which many different types of sports were valued equally and a variety of types of people could succeed. Then the effort exerted by a tall, skinny long-distance runner and a short, bulky hockey player would be appreciated equally—whether the athletes were boys or girls.

BILLIE JEAN KING AND THE BATTLE OF THE SEXES

The year was 1973. More than 30,000 people were crammed into the Houston Astrodome. Many waved brightly colored banners, and their excited shouts filled the air. At the same time, all over the world, 50 million more people turned on their televisions. A historic event was about to take place. Everybody wanted to watch. What event had so many people so excited? Was it the Super Bowl or the World Series? No. It was a tennis match between two Wimbledon champions: Bobby Riggs and Billie Jean King.

As the band launched into a bold tune, the players entered the arena. From one side came Bobby Riggs, a 55-year-old professional athlete who was known as one of the cleverest players in tennis. Billie Jean King made a grand entrance. Waving her racket and riding in a feather-covered Egyptian litter, the 30-year-old Wimbledon and U.S. Open champion looked like a winner. But would she be victorious in this real-life battle of the sexes?

The controversy had started when Bobby Riggs issued a challenge. "You say that women provide a brand of tennis equal to men," he once said to Billie Jean King. "Well, prove it. I say that you not only can-

not beat a top male pro, you cannot even beat a tired old man like me."

King didn't let Riggs' teasing get the best of her. She was a great athlete. She didn't need to be part of some crazy publicity stunt, so she turned him down. But then Margaret Court, another tennis great, accepted Riggs' challenge. Riggs beat her, and he boasted, "Any man can beat any woman. Women always choke."

When Riggs challenged King again, this time offering $100,000 in prize money, she told him she'd take him on. Even though she was much younger than Riggs, many observers thought King could never win the match. Tennis star Arthur Ashe told reporters, "Bobby will jerk Billie Jean around so much she'll look like a yo-yo."

King was no tennis amateur. Ranked as the number one player in the world, she had been winning at Wimbledon since age 17. Her powerful playing and outspoken support for women's rights had made her one of the most talked-about athletes of all time.

Once the dramatic entrances were over, the match began. Almost from the beginning, King kept Riggs running from one end of the court to the other, beating him easily. "The Bat-

Billie Jean King and Bobby Riggs vigorously promoted the "Battle of the Sexes."

tle of the Sexes" was over. Billie Jean King had won.

But was everyone convinced? After her victory, King continued to fight for equal prize money and recognition for women players. Now that the whole world had watched her play a man and win, King was convinced that people would soon learn to take women's tennis seri-ously. All they had to do was watch. She once said, "I believed that if women were worth anything, then we could somehow convince people to come and watch us play."

Sources: George Sullivan, *Great Lives: Sports* (Charles Scribner's Sons: New York, 1988); Billie Jean King with Frank Deford, *Billie Jean* (Viking Press: New York, 1982).

CHAPTER TWO

BEING A WINNER

What if someone told you there was a magic potion that would make you healthier, stronger, more successful, and more self-confident? Would you try it? What if you discovered that this magic potion was easy to find? Now imagine the potion was fun to take and contained no drugs. Sound too good to be true? One activity *can* provide all these benefits and more. That magic potion is sports, and as more girls and women are becoming active, researchers are discovering the ways sports participation can make life better for anyone.

"I grew up playing sports, and I think being active helped my self-confidence," said Kelley Owen, a member of the U.S. women's national hockey team. "Being good at sports can help any girl feel better about herself, and playing on a team helps build character."

A 1992 study conducted by the Melpomene Institute, titled *Girls' Perspectives: Physical Activity and Self-Esteem,* found evidence to support Owen's claims. A research team interviewed 76 geographically, racially, and economically diverse 9- to 12-year-old girls, and found that the girls who were

Girls can boost their self-esteem by participating in sports.

physically active had higher levels of self-esteem than the girls who were not. The study also found that girls who began playing sports at a young age were more likely to be physically active as they got older.[1]

"My sense is that developing athletic skills at an early age gives girls an extra sense of self-confidence that helps them throughout their lives," explained Lynn Jaffee, co-author of the Melpomene report. "Feeling confident growing up helps girls feel comfortable taking risks as they become women."

Professional firefighter Andrea Minkinen says growing up playing sports with her father and brothers helped give her the confidence she needed to become the first female firefighter in her city. "Sports enhance everything I do," she said. "I think being athletic all my life made it easy for me to do the type of work I do."

Chris Voelz, University of Minnesota women's athletic director, says her active childhood has helped her feel confident and secure as an adult. "Being in sports . . . raises girls' self-esteem by teaching them that they can get in there and wrestle with the boys, but that they don't have to

BOYS, GIRLS, AND SPORTS

Statistics show that after age 13, fewer and fewer girls participate in sports, while boys' levels of participation remain much the same throughout their high school years. Why does this happen?

One study, conducted by the Melpomene Institute, asked girls ages 9-12 to tell about times they felt uncomfortable playing or participating in sports. The study found that girls often felt reluctant to play sports with boys who weren't family members or neighborhood friends because they were afraid of "being criticized by the boys with whom they were playing."

One girl said, "Sometimes the boys don't want to give you the ball and you feel like, 'Am I doing something wrong?' But probably they just don't want to give me the ball because I'm bad." Another girl said she likes to play games, but hates it when the boys tease her. "When I play with the boys, if you miss the ball they'll start kind of yelling at you and they get mad at you," she said. "So it makes me uncomfortable to play with them when they do that."

Another girl said when she plays with boys, they tell her what to do and how to play. It makes her angry, she said. "Well, sometimes I like playing sports, but there's someone I don't like and he's criticizing me all the time and saying, 'Oh, you can't do that.' And he's always stealing my ball and stuff, so I just put my ball away," she said.

"Boys are a huge barrier to girls taking risks," said Lynn Jaffee, co-author of the report. "Even as early as grade school, boys control the game. They are in charge, and they don't pass to girls. There is a general assumption that being a girl automatically means you're a bad athlete."

How can adults encourage girls to become athletes? One way, said Jaffee, is to make girls feel confident in their abilities by encouraging them to participate in sports at an early age.

"The younger a girl starts being athletic, the more comfortable she will be with her body," Jaffee said. "The more comfortable and confident a girl feels, the more likely she will continue to participate in sports."

Also, author Mariah Burton Nelson contends that as boys see more women and girls compete in sports, either in real life or on television, they appreciate the effort and skills of female athletes. They grow to respect them as athletes.

Sources: Interviews with Kathryn Reith and Lynn Jaffee; Mariah Burton Nelson, *The Stronger Women Get, the More Men Love Football, Sexism and the American Culture of Sports (*New York: Harcourt Brace and Company, 1994); Lynn Jaffee and Rebecca Manzer, "Girls' Perspectives: Physical Activity and Self-Esteem," *Melpomene Journal,* 1992.

give up being women in order to be athletic," she said.

Harvard researcher Carol Gilligan talked to hundreds of young girls about self-esteem. She found that girls tend to feel best about themselves during pre-adolescence—before the onset of puberty brings drastic physical and emotional changes and societal expectations. Gilligan found that after puberty girls tend to see themselves as less able, more awkward, and less worthy than boys. She said contact with strong adult female role models and a constant involvement in athletic activities can help counter these feelings of insecurity and inadequacy and prepare girls for the adult world.[2]

Being athletic also helps girls

and women feel more comfortable with their bodies. Dr. Kay Porter, owner of the Eugene, Oregon, sports and organization counseling firm Porter Foster, surveyed 218 of the runners in a 1979 10-kilometer women's race. She analyzed their comments about depression, anxiety, relationship satisfaction, and safety. More than 90 percent of the runners Porter interviewed said that running had increased their positive self-image and made them feel better about their bodies.[3]

Olympic heptathlete Jackie Joyner-Kersee grew up playing sports with her brother, Al. She tells fans that her active, healthy lifestyle has given her confidence in her abilities and pride in her body. "I love myself," the gold medalist once said.[4]

ACADEMIC ACHIEVEMENT

Forget everything you've ever heard about dumb athletes. Researchers have found that the stereotypical muscle-brained jock—the one who'd rather spend time in the gym than the classroom—is rare. In fact, studies seem to show that athletic activity actually improves most students' classroom performance.

Jackie Joyner-Kersee competes in the heptathlon, a seven-event contest that includes the 100-meter hurdles race, high jump, shot put, 200-meters race, long jump, javelin throw, and 800-meters run.

In the 1980s, the Women's Sports Foundation conducted a four-year study of more than 30,000 high school boys and girls. After examining the students' test scores, monitoring their extracurricular activities, and conducting private interviews, researchers discovered that varsity athletes were more likely than nonathletes to "score well on achievement tests, report high popularity, stay in high school, attend college and seek a bachelor's degree."[5]

Chris Voelz said that lessons learned in athletics, like being a good sport and working as part of a team, are skills that can help athletes become better students. "Sports hold you accountable," Voelz once said. "They teach you to take responsibility, teach you to build a safety net for failure, to work for a common goal instead of concentrating on yourself. Sports teach you to work under pressure. They teach you that you can compete and win."

Tennis champion Althea Gib-

son was one young woman whose academic life improved when she became involved in athletics. Growing up poor on the rough streets of New York City, Gibson hated school and often skipped classes. Eventually, she even

Althea Gibson won the U.S. Open and Wimbledon championships in 1957 and 1958.

dropped out of high school. When she started taking tennis lessons at a local club, Gibson's outlook changed. She was always good at tennis, and playing the game made her feel like she could do anything she wanted. Soon Gibson went back to high school, made friends, and graduated near the top of her class. "I was determined that I was going to be somebody—if it killed me," she once said.[6]

CAREER SUCCESS

When Lynn Olson was growing up, she loved sports. She loved running and jumping, but she especially loved skating. She never suspected that one day her athletic interests would help her become the first woman ever to sit on the board of directors at USA Hockey. "It was wonderful," she said. "The skills I learned in sports helped me compete and succeed in the business world."

Besides gaining more immediate benefits like good health and academic achievement, many successful women report that being athletic while they were growing up helped them succeed in business. Minkinen, the firefighter, holds a second-degree

black belt in karate. Growing up, she played basketball, baseball, and football at home. In school she was a cheerleader. She says the self-confidence and competition skills she learned as a young athlete helped her find jobs and succeed in those jobs where other women had failed.

"In sports, I learned about competition," Minkinen said. "Growing up, most girls don't learn how to compete, and when they're confronted with a competitive situation at work, they just don't know what to do. I learned how to handle failure and roll with the punches."

Kelley Owen said the teamwork skills she uses on the hockey rink also work well in her professional life. Cooperating with other people and concentrating on a common goal rather than individual concerns helped her move beyond "the small stuff" to be the best worker she could be.

"I know how to be a team player, and that has helped me succeed," Owen said. "You can be the best athlete in the world, but if your team's no good, you'll never get anywhere."

In their book, *The Sporting Woman*, Mary A. Boutilier and Lucinda SanGiovanni propose

that "sport is a microcosm of society, reflecting the basic values, beliefs, rules, and ideas of the larger system." In other words, the skills athletes learn playing sports are the very skills our society requires for success. "In both the larger society and in sport," they write, "primary importance" is placed on such values as "competition and success, hard work, striving, and deferred gratification, progress, materialism, . . . and external conformity."

For years, boys learned these values on playing fields and in gyms, while girls, for the most part, were told that these were the very characteristics they should avoid. "The composite picture" of the ideal athletic citizen, Boutilier and SanGiovanni conclude, was "the red-blooded, wholesome, virile man, one sound in body and mind . . . guided by self-discipline and the competitive spirit . . . successful in sport and in other social endeavors."[7]

Teach young women these values and you've got a recipe for success, said Dorothy McIntyre, associate executive director of the Minnesota State High School League. When women begin making strides in athletics, they begin to move forward in the professional world, she said. The corporate world often operates like the sports world, McIntyre said. Competition, teamwork, assertiveness, and self-confidence are skills and traits she prizes in both athletes and co-workers.

"I'm seeing more and more of that in women," she said. "And I think the next generation of young women will be even stronger and more confident than the last. A lot of today's successful women owe at least part of their success to sports and sports participation."

BABE DIDRIKSON

Her name was Mildred Ella Didrikson, but everybody called her Babe. She often boasted she could run faster and jump higher than anyone, and she was usually right. "I can beat anyone I set my mind to," she was fond of saying. Once, when she competed in a track meet, she told the other runners: "I'm going to win everything I enter," and she nearly did.

Babe Didrikson was born in 1911 in Port Arthur, Texas. The youngest daughter of Norwegian immigrants, she excelled at sports almost from the moment she could walk. Her parents moved to Beaumont, Texas, when she was young. She raced streetcars there, trying to beat them from stop to stop along the street.

At home, Babe challenged the neighbor children to games in her backyard. Fiercely competitive, she could kick a football farther and throw a baseball harder than any boy in town. Her nickname was Babe because her home-run record reminded the other children of their baseball hero, Babe Ruth.

In high school, Babe played on every girls' team. She hated dresses and skirts, and came to school dressed in her brothers' old clothes. Some girls made fun of her appearance and her athletic ways, but if

Mildred "Babe" Didrikson

Babe cared, she never let it show. She concentrated on sports, starring on every single team.

The local newspapers printed stories about the "girl wonder." One night a talent scout from Dallas came to one of Babe's basketball games. He was looking for players for a touring women's basketball team called the Golden Cyclones. When he saw Babe play, he wanted her on the team! Joining the Golden Cyclones meant dropping out of high school, but Babe persuaded her parents to let her quit school and move to Dallas. Once there, Babe became the Cyclones' star forward.

Soon Babe's bragging got on the other players' nerves. She was younger than most of them, and she was fond of boasting about her athletic achievements. Because she was the team's best player, the owners gave her a raise. The rest of the players' salaries remained the same, even after the team won second place at the Amateur Athletic Union (AAU) national women's basketball tournament. Babe only thinks about winning, the other players complained. She's too confident for her own good.

But the Cyclones' coach, Melvorne J. McCombs, found Babe's self-confidence inspiring. She was the best athlete he had ever seen—

woman or man. He knew she had the determination and drive it takes to be a true champion. Now all she needed was a sport with more opportunities. McCombs introduced her to track and field.

Babe loved track and field from the moment she went to her first meet. Running and jumping reminded her of backyard games in Beaumont. Soon she started winning almost every event she entered.

With each new medal, Babe's confidence grew. She was selected for the 1932 Olympic track team. For Babe, competing in the Olympics was a dream come true. "I'm the greatest!" she told her Olympic teammates. "No one's better than me!" And she was right. Babe won a medal in every event she entered, returning to Texas with two golds and a silver. People in Dallas held a big parade in her honor.

Babe's career didn't end at the Olympics. She was a lifelong athlete.

In 1933, after a brief career in vaudeville (she ran on a treadmill, sang, and played the harmonica), she became a professional golfer.

She married professional wrestler George Zaharias in 1938, and he became her manager. In 1946, she won 17 tournaments in a row. Sportswriters and fans called her the "World's Greatest Woman Athlete," but Babe was unimpressed. "I could've told them that myself," she said.

Babe died of cancer in 1956. She was 45 years old.

Source: R. R. Knudson, *Babe Didrikson: Athlete of the Century* (New York: Viking Kestrel, 1985).

CHAPTER THREE

OFF THE SIDELINES

■

Maria Pepe wanted to play baseball and, in 1972, that was a problem. Maria was 11. She'd been playing ball in Hoboken, New Jersey, since she was 5. Just like all the boys she played with every day, she wanted to join the local Little League team. But no girl had ever been on a team before.

Maria's parents agreed to let her join a team, and the team's coach approved. But when national Little League officials found out, they tried to keep Maria from playing. Baseball is traditionally a boys' game, they said, because boys are stronger, better athletes than girls. They claimed that to admit girls would cripple the Little League program.

Maria's family refused to give in. Girls, they argued, had just as much right to play baseball as boys. They took the case to court. Two years later, after much discussion in the courts and in the legislature, girls were allowed to play baseball on Little League teams. The courts found, in part, that "8- to 12-year-old females, on the average, are about two years ahead of comparably aged males in physical, bone, and hormonal development." Because girls are

Maria Pepe's love for baseball motivated her to take on national Little League officials when they told her she couldn't play.

more physically advanced than boys, the courts found no reason to believe that boys and girls couldn't play sports together. By the time the court decided that girls could play baseball with boys, Maria was 13—too old to play in Little League. But the next year, 50 girls enrolled in the Hoboken Little League program.[1]

Maria Pepe wasn't the only girl who fought to play on boys' teams in the 1960s and 1970s. The American feminist movement was heating up, and women and men across the country were working to pass laws designed to bring about equality between the sexes. These activists said that people, no matter what their gender, were entitled to equal rights and equal protection under the law. Giving girls the same athletic opportunities as boys was considered an important step toward equality. As women began to demand and defend their rights, the issue of providing sports for girls in public schools was debated.

Inspired by trailblazers like Maria Pepe, more girls joined the movement. "When my fifth-grade physical education teacher said that boys would play basketball and girls would skip rope, I became a basketball activist," said basketball coach and record-holder Janet Karvonen.[2]

When school officials said girls and women were too weak to participate in sports alongside men and boys, feminists disagreed, pointing to the accomplishments of such athletes as Babe Didrikson, Billie Jean King, and Wilma Rudolph. If they can do it, so can we, they said. Sports would never be the same.

TITLE IX

Maria Pepe's case and others like it became the foundation for a law called Title IX. Passed by Congress in 1972 as part of the Educational Amendment Act to the 1964

Civil Rights Act, Title IX changed the history of American sports forever. The law read, in part:

"... no person in the United States shall, on the basis of sex, be excluded from participation in, be denied the benefits of, or be subjected to discrimination under any educational program or activity receiving financial or federal assistance."

In other words, Title IX made it illegal for schools that receive federal money to offer an activity to students of one gender but not the other. As far as sports were concerned, schools didn't have to offer exactly the same sports to girls and boys, but they did have to provide equal athletic opportunities for both, including an equal number of teams.

Elementary schools were supposed to comply with Title IX regulations by 1976, and high schools and colleges were told to comply by 1978. Making more sports available greatly increased girls' participation in athletics. In the 20 years after Title IX was enacted, the number of girls playing on teams increased dramatically. In 1971, fewer than 300,000 girls played high school sports. By 1990, 1.9 million did.[3]

While Title IX was a great step

forward for women and girls, the law didn't solve every problem or remove every inequity. In a few cases, complying with Title IX actually made things worse for women in sports. Providing equal athletic opportunities can be expensive, and some schools needed to cut existing boys' teams in order to start new teams for girls. Replacing boys' teams with girls' teams made some people angry. Girls aren't interested in sports, these people said, and not many people come to their games anyway.

Even though more girls than ever play on school teams, boys still outnumber girls 2 to 1 in sports participation. Making more sports available to girls doesn't always mean people will accept girls playing "traditionally boys'" sports, either. A recent study of Michigan high school students found that young people still hold on to old prejudices when it comes to athletic activity. When asked to list male sports, study participants wrote down nearly every sport offered in their schools. Female sports, on the other hand, included only figure skating, gymnastics, jump rope, and cheerleading.[4]

Before Title IX was enacted, 90

percent of women's college athletic programs were run by women. By 1992, the number had dropped to 48 percent.[5] The reason? Because Title IX required equal opportunities for men and women, many schools merged athletic departments in order to save money. More often than not, male directors (who had been working at these jobs much longer than their female counterparts) were put in charge of the newly merged department, and women directors lost their jobs.

Girls' high school programs suffered as well. In Minnesota in 1972, for instance, 98 percent of the coaches of girls' high school teams were women. Fifteen years after the passage of Title IX, that figure had declined to 33 percent. A number of factors led to the loss of women in high school coaching positions. University of Minnesota researcher Kimberly Ann Olson studied the changing profile of high school coaches. She concluded, in part, that "Title IX made girls' sports more prestigious and brought about equitable salaries for coaches. As a result, men became more interested in coaching girls' sports." Also, Olson said that some early women coaches may have left be-

Chris Voelz, University of Minnesota women's athletic director

cause they were not "trained as coaches and had been coaching to fill a void."[6]

But Chris Voelz, director of the University of Minnesota's women's athletic department (one of the few independent women's college departments), said Title IX has changed women's lives for the better. "Twenty years ago, athletic women were tomboys and that was about it," Voelz said. "Now

THE BIG GAME

On January 30, 1993, thousands of people came to Nashville, Tennessee. They didn't come to town for a country-western concert or a parade or a speech. They came to watch a basketball game, and they became a part of history.

Now, if it had been a men's basketball game, the crowds wouldn't have seemed too unusual. But the game that took place that night was a *women's* basketball game between the Commodores of Vanderbilt University and the Lady Vols of the University of Tennessee.

According to *Sports Illustrated,* this game was the first women's basketball game ever to be sold out weeks in advance. Nashville's Memorial Gym was filled to its capacity of 15,317. More than 1,000 people had to be turned away. U.S. women's college basketball has a history of low attendance figures. Before the January 30 game, for instance, the Vanderbilt Commodores' average home game attendance was only 3,542.

Many of the spectators in Nashville had never been to a women's game before. Special promotions helped attract them. Television and radio stations had broadcast promotional announcements, and local newspapers and magazines had printed stories. This game was the first matchup between No. 1 and No. 2 women's teams that were from the same state. Vice President Al Gore, who grew up in Tennessee, bragged to reporters, "It's not surprising that the top two ranked women's basketball teams are from Tennessee."

"It's almost more important to play well (than to win)," Vanderbilt center Heidi Gillingham told a sports reporter. "With so many fans, many of whom are testing out women's basketball to see if they like it, we need to show them the high level at which women can play. We need to convince them they should come back."

The game was skillful, exciting, and fast-paced. The score was nail-bitingly close throughout most of the game. Tennessee came from behind in the last 10 seconds to win 73-68. "The game and the event were worthy of each other," wrote *Sports Illustrated* reporter Phil Taylor. The matchup drew the attention of sportswriters, athletes,

and fans although, unlike important college men's games, it wasn't broadcast on national TV. Tennessee coach Pat Summit told reporters, "That was a terrific environment for both teams, for women's basketball. What made it exciting was the crowd. I'd love to play in that environment every night."

Source: Phil Taylor, "Music City Madness," *Sports Illustrated,* February 8, 1983.

Steffi Graf was the top-ranked player in women's tennis from August 1987 to March 1991—the longest stretch one woman has ever held the top ranking.

'tomboys' can be sports heroes and role models for young girls ready to discover the great opportunities sports can bring them."

FUNDING INEQUITIES

We've all heard the story. A poor kid grows up in the tough part of town. Life is rough, but the kid has a dream. One day, the kid says, I'm going to get out of here. I'm going to be the best football (or basketball or baseball) player in school, and I'll win a college scholarship. Then I'll go pro. Nice story, right? The plot varies and very few kids actually become professional athletes, but one element of this story remains the same. The kid is always a boy.

Even though half of all students enrolled in American undergraduate programs are women, less than 33 percent of athletic scholarship dollars are awarded to female athletes. The money colleges spend to recruit promising young women isn't nearly as much money as they spend on recruiting men. Only 18 percent of college recruiting budgets are spent on women's sports.[7]

A female athlete's chance of going on to professional sports is very slim. Nearly every major U.S. city has at least one professional men's team. Women's professional sports, however, are virtually nonexistent, except for tennis, golf, bowling, and beach volleyball.

"Growing up, girls receive these subtle, covert messages that what we do as athletes doesn't count," Voelz said. "When so many more dollars get spent on men than on women, we are getting the message that women's sports aren't nearly as important as men's are."

Big, sports-oriented schools often spend their recruiting budgets courting prospective male athletes. The most talented prospects are offered all-expenses-paid scholarships, free athletic clothing, and help with their studies. Coaches from top schools often battle over the best recruits, raising their scholarship offer whenever their rivals make a new offer.

Voelz and her colleagues at the University of Minnesota say they aren't interested in spending large amounts of recruitment money on promising female athletes: They just want the money more evenly distributed. "To tell the truth," Voelz said, "I don't think we need to match the men's recruit-

Amy Alcott, who joined the Ladies' Professional Golf Association tour when she was 19, has won five major titles and more than $2.9 million.

ing expenses. But I think we need to be able to spend enough money on our athletes, and both departments need to take a closer

look at the money they use, and ask 'Is this well spent?'"

The money has to come from somewhere. At most schools, when a women's or girls' sport is given additional funding, money must be taken away from a men's or boys' sport. This causes controversy among coaches, players, and fans.

Only 1 of the 107 Division I-A colleges was meeting the Title IX standard by 1993. Washington State University's student population in 1993 was 46 percent female. The university's student-athlete population was 44 percent female. "We were dragged kicking and screaming into the forefront," said Washington State associate athletic director Harold C. Gibson, referring to a Washington State Supreme Court ruling. "People thought the sky was falling."[8]

Christine Grant, women's athletic director at the University of Iowa, told *Chicago Tribune* reporter Ed Sherman that she thinks the tradeoff is necessary. Women's athletic departments are simply looking to "level the playing field," she said, even if that means that some men's teams will suffer. "I feel the institutions should have moved in the last 20 years," Grant said. "Schools have

Christine Grant, University of Iowa women's athletic director

had 20 years to think about this. It's unfortunate for the young men who get cut, but it's even more unfortunate for the millions of young women who have missed out for 100 years. Somebody has to say that."[9]

Bob Darden, the men's gymnastics coach at Michigan, argues that it does nobody any good to take opportunities away from some athletes just to give them to others. "Based on history, affirmative action identifies a disadvantaged segment of society and empowers someone to eliminate what's occurred," Darden told Sherman. "But to disadvantage someone else in the process is not fair."[10]

Football is usually the biggest drain on any college's sports budget. A Division I-A football team gives about 92 scholarships, and the coaching staff's salaries cost about $500,000 a year. A typical team has as many as 145 players, while National Football League teams have 47.[11]

Some experts recommend limiting football recruiting budgets, reducing the number of players on a team, and cutting the length of preseason football practices. But others, like former Auburn University football coach Pat Dye, argue against those limits. At many big schools, football draws more players, spectators, and brings in more money than any other sport. Women are well-served by the sports opportunities available to them now, Dye says. Why mess with a good thing? "To tell a kid he can't come out for college football as a walk-on because it creates a numbers problem with the women in another area, I mean that's almost like communism. That isn't what this country was built on, or what it stands for," he said.[12]

AT THE HELM

In 1990 Bernadette Locke-Mattox became the first woman to be a part of the coaching staff of a major men's college basketball team. Locke-Mattox was the assistant coach of the Kentucky Wildcats until 1993, when she became an administrator in the athletic department.

A former All-American at the University of Georgia, Locke-Mattox knows basketball, and she's not afraid to keep male players in line. "Lack of effort bends me out of shape," she said.

The Wildcat players say they respect Locke-Mattox. She pushes them to keep up their grade point averages, while insisting they play the best game they can.

She sees no problem with a woman coaching men. "Any coach who is capable of coaching can do anything he or she wants," she once said. "Just like if you're a great teacher, you can teach anywhere."

Source: William Plummer, "Women among Wildcats," *People,* March 22, 1993, pp. 51-52.

FOSTERING RESPECT

Turn on the TV set. Have you ever noticed the differences between men's and women's college basketball games? Go beyond the details, like smaller basketballs, longer shot clocks, and the way the players move on the court. Look at the crowds. Men's college games are usually packed with cheering fans waving banners and wearing team colors. Women's games draw smaller crowds, though the fans' devotion remains as strong. "Men's games draw bigger crowds," Chris Voelz said. "This may be because schools put more emphasis on the achievements and skills of their men's teams."

Move your attention from the stands to the scoreboard. While men's teams often have tough-sounding names like Bulldogs, Demons, and Rebels, women's teams are given softer names. This is usually accomplished by adding the word "Lady" to the original team name. Thus the Bulldogs become the Lady Bulldogs, the Demons the Lady Demons—you get the picture.

"The message is clear," said sports sociologist Mary Jo Kane. "We are ladies first and athletes second." This feminizing of women's teams is degrading, Kane said. "It tells the world that it's much more important to be a 'lady' than a good athlete."

Finally, think about how the players are portrayed. Sports sociologist Margaret Carlisle Duncan studied 186 photographs from the 1984 and 1988 Olympics for the *Sociology of Sport Journal.* She found that the photographs were more likely to show female athletes displaying emotions or crying, while male athletes were more often portrayed as active and dominant. "Camera angles typically focus up to male athletes and down on female athletes," Duncan wrote.[13]

These elements combine to create a dismal state of affairs for women athletes. But Kane says there's still hope for the future.

This image of Mary Decker in tears after falling in the 3,000-meter race at the 1984 Olympics captured the attention of sports fans. Some thought that showing Decker, the U.S. 3,000-meters champion, crying trivialized her accomplishments.

"While there's no doubt that sexism reigns in the world of college sports, women have made some significant accomplishments," Kane said. "Look at where women were 20 years ago. We have made tremendous strides."

GIRLS' ATHLETIC ASSOCIATION

Imagine that your school's sports roster included football, baseball, basketball, hockey, tennis, swimming, and track. You were good at sports, had been playing them all your life. You wanted to join a team, but couldn't. Imagine that the only reason you couldn't be on a team was that you were a girl.

In the first half of this century, most public schools in the United States didn't offer any varsity sports for girls. Athletic activities were thought to be unladylike and even unhealthy for girls.

In the late 1950s and early 1960s, many junior highs and high schools formed Girls' Athletic Associations, or GAAs. A loosely organized network of girls' intramural (within school) teams, the GAA was a way for schools to give girls the opportunity to participate in extracurricular athletics.

Through GAA, a variety of sports were made available to girls, including tennis, basketball, volleyball, and softball. Games and practices usually took place after school, but special sporting events called "play days" were occasionally held on weekends.

By the early 1970s, GAA had helped many girls become more interested in sports. In some states, girls' high school basketball got its start through the GAA. Girls who would otherwise never have played team sports were given an opportunity through GAA programs.

Many girls enjoyed the new athletic opportunities GAA offered them, but some felt the program also had its drawbacks. Because it was still widely believed that girls were weaker than boys, the GAA used a different set of playing rules. The GAA rules changed the way games were played. For instance, players passed more and ran less in girls rules basketball. Girls were even required to take frequent cookie and juice breaks so they wouldn't get too tired.

Some girls found that the new rules slowed down the action and made organized sports less enjoyable than those that they played with other boys and girls. "Girls rules were boring," said one woman who grew up playing GAA sports. "It was sad because we wanted to

run and move fast, and they wanted us to stand still."

Another drawback of GAA was the way it made girls' sports seem less important than boys' sports. While boys' teams wore uniforms, starred at pep rallies, and traveled by bus to out-of-town games, GAA teams wore colored cloth pinafores (called pinnies) instead of uniforms, competed alone in empty gyms, and often didn't have coaches or equipment.

The GAA also discouraged competition, citing scientific evidence from prominent national organizations like the American Physical Education Association: "There is widespread agreement that girls should not be exposed to extremes of fatigue or strain, either emotional or physical . . . . In addition, custom and good taste should always influence in questions of public display, costumes, publicity."

For these reasons, many girls felt limited by the GAA. "We wanted to run," said another former GAA member, "but the GAA only let us walk." By the late 1970s, even before Title IX called for more opportunities for girls, most schools had cancelled their GAA programs.

Sources: Minnesota State High School League booklet, and interviews with Janet Kordonowy and Jennifer Tongen.

CHAPTER FOUR

PRO DREAMS

■

Pro basketball superstar Michael Jordan makes millions of dollars every year in salary and endorsements. Shoes, clothing, cereal boxes, books, and posters bearing his likeness are sold all over the world. Magic Johnson is also a celebrity. He lives in a big house and drives fancy cars, spending money he earned during his successful professional basketball career.

Though not every professional basketball player is as famous as Jordan or Johnson, most earn large salaries, and many make much more than a million dollars a year. Professional sports are popular in the United States, and owners pay top prices to lure the best players to their teams. If the players are male, that is.

"Salaries for male athletes are really getting out of line," said Kathryn Reith, former communications director for the Women's Sports Foundation. "But the biggest outrage is that these men are making exorbitant wages, while equally talented women can't find any opportunities to play professionally in the United States. I see an imbalance there."

Many observers argue that

Martina Navratilova, who retired in 1994, is the only female tennis player to have won nine Wimbledon singles titles.

high-profile male athletes earn their big salaries. Sports sociologist Harry Edwards, in his book *Sociology of Sport,* said modern athletes are entertainers, and big salaries are part of the game. "Clearly sport rests on an economic foundation," he wrote.[1]

American women have very few opportunities to earn a living in professional sports (though some outstanding athletes, like basketball player Nancy Lieberman-Cline, have been able to earn good salaries through professional leagues and endorsements). While some of the most talented young male athletes can look forward to a career playing their favorite game, females must often look elsewhere for professional opportunities. The game of basketball is a good example.

FAR AND AWAY

Women's professional basketball teams have been launched in the United States before, but the efforts have been unsuccessful: None lasted more than a few years. For example, the eight-team Women's Basketball League lasted from 1978 until 1982.

Other women's leagues were more successful. Women played professional baseball in the All American Girls Professional Baseball League (AAGPBL) from 1943-1952. Baseball promoters originally formed the women's teams during World War II after the male players went to war. The AAGPBL games drew large crowds, and the teams continued even after the men came home. Eventually, though, the AAGPBL was disbanded.

There are some women's professional leagues, including beach volleyball, golf, and tennis, but a women's pro basketball league doesn't exist in the United States. In an article published in *The Sporting News,* sports reporter Lisa Dillman wrote: "The NCAA Tournament is virtually the final opportunity for the American public to see the nation's best female players on the court."[2] Because opportunities in the United States are slim, the best women's collegiate players are left with two choices, Dillman says. They can leave the sport or leave the country.

Leaving the country is a realistic option. Professional women's basketball teams are successful in other countries, including Japan, Italy, Spain, Sweden, and France. Foreign coaches recruit promising Americans for high-paying jobs.

The All American Girls Professional Baseball League emphasized femininity, but the players often concentrated more on how they played than on how they looked.

Beach volleyball is one of the newest professional sports opportunities for women.

"These are my best years," said Teresa Edwards, a member of the 1992 U.S. women's Olympic bas-ketball team who has played pro-fessionally in Japan. "I'm so much better now than in college. And if

I hadn't gone away, I'd have lost my talent."[3]

The best American women often become celebrities in their adopted countries, but many say they wish they didn't have to move so far away to play basketball. "I hope there's a U.S. women's league someday," said two-time Olympian Cynthia Cooper.[4]

Some athletes think that women's sports are popular in foreign countries partly because both men's and women's teams were introduced with equal fanfare. Foreign men's leagues aren't as overwhelmingly popular as they are in the United States. In Europe and Asia, female players are celebrities, and they are promoted and advertised enthusiastically. "I'm a professional, and in Europe I'm treated that way," said Bridgette Gordon, an American who plays pro basketball in Italy. "I'm used to being a star."[5]

But foreign opportunities for women athletes are shrinking. The Japanese teams recently announced that foreign players will no longer be allowed to play. This means that high profile American women like Teresa Edwards, Medina Dixon, and Venus Lacy will have to look for new jobs.[6]

Teresa Edwards led the U.S. women's basketball team to Olympic gold medals in 1984 and 1988. The United States won the bronze medal in 1992.

Billie Jean King led the drive to award female tennis pros prize money equal to that of male players. King won six Wimbledon singles titles in the 1960s and 1970s.

Some professional sports in America offer nearly as many opportunities for women as for men. Women tennis pros make almost as much or more than their male counterparts: In 1981, Martina Navratilova earned $865,437 in prize money; John McEnroe made $991,000. In 1983 Navratilova made history. She earned $6,089,756—the most ever earned in one year by any tennis player, male or female.[7]

Successful female tennis professionals have Billie Jean King to thank for their financial opportunities. When she first started playing tennis in the 1960s, King saw that men's tournament prizes were much larger than women's. (For example, the Pacific Southwest Championships offered $12,000 to the winning man and $1,500 to the winning woman.) King didn't think it was fair that men earned more money than women. She was playing hard, winning Wimbledon finals, and yet she was forced to get by on $100 a week. Male players—some who weren't nearly as talented as she was—were able to live comfortably on their prize money.

In 1973 King recruited Navratilova, Chris Evert, and other women tennis stars, and they

Gabriela Sabatini is just one of the professional players who benefit from Billie Jean King's efforts.

LYNETTE WOODARD

For nearly 40 years, the Harlem Globetrotters have dazzled specta-tors with their skillful playing, their bright red, white, and blue uni-forms, and their hilarious antics. More than 100 million fans worldwide have seen them play in exhibition matches. Some say they are the world's best-known basketball team. In 1985 the Globetrot-ters did something that made them even more famous. They signed Lynette Woodard, making her the first female Globetrotter and the first woman to play alongside men on a professional basketball team.

Before joining the Globetrotters, Woodard was a standout for the Kansas University Jayhawks and co-captain of the 1984 women's Olympic basketball team. She was unstoppable on the court. Coaches and officials liked her, too. She was the first woman ever to be given a NCAA Top Five award, an award honoring the top five col-lege basketball players in the country.

After her college graduation, Lynette wanted to continue playing basketball, but there were no professional leagues for women in the United States. She moved to Italy and joined a professional team there. "I love this game so much I want to keep playing," she said.

Woodard had a dream. She wanted to play for the Harlem Globe-trotters. "When you play basketball, you go on the court and fanta-size about being different players," she once said. "The Globetrotters were the team I thought about all the time." Woodard's dream came true in 1985 when the Globetrotters asked her and 20 other female players to try out. The competition was intense, but Woodard was selected for the team. The tryouts had been rough and Woodard told reporters she was afraid she might not be selected.

Woodard played for the Globetrotters until 1987. "I don't know how long it will take," she once told a writer, "but a woman will play in the NBA. I want people to see me play with the Globetrotters and say a woman could also have the ability to play in the NBA."

Sources: Ruth M. Sparhawk, *American Women in Sport, 1887-1987: A 100-year Chronology,* (The Scarecrow Press: New Jersey, 1989) and Matthew Newman, *Lynette Woodard* (Crestwood House: Minnesota, 1986).

formed a players' union called the Women's Tennis Association. The WTA members threatened to boycott major tournaments until women's awards equaled men's. Tournament promoters gave in.[8]

King has said that money isn't everything, but in the world of professional sports, how much money athletes make is a measure of their success and achievement. "Money is opportunity and security," she once told a reporter.[9] Compared to modern tennis players, King's income was never high, but the doors of opportunity she pushed open will never again be shut. In 1990 *Life* magazine named her one of the 100 most important Americans of the 20th century. "And I haven't even started yet," she said.[10]

ON THE SIDELINES

Tune your radio to your favorite sports event. Listen to the announcer. Is the voice you hear male or female? Now turn on the television set. Flip to a football, basketball, hockey, or baseball game. Watch the nightly news. Who reports sports events? Who analyzes, comments, and describes most games? Are the faces you see male or female? Count the bylines you see at the top of most sports stories in newspapers and magazines. Which kind of names do you see more often? Male or female?

The answer to most of these questions is male. Sports reporting is a mostly male profession, as are other sports support jobs like officiating and coaching. Why are the names and faces associated with professional sports so often male? Sports sociologist Mary Jo Kane says that because society considers athletics a male pastime—something not suitable for females—women who attempt to break into that closed world often face resistance. "It can range from subtle harassment to worse," Kane said. "Many talented women get frightened away."

For years, female reporters were banned from conducting locker room interviews. We have a right to privacy, the players said, and we don't want women interviewing us when we are getting undressed. Male reporters, on the other hand, were allowed to enter most locker rooms, even those of female athletes. Either ban all reporters, the female journalists demanded, or let us in. The men are getting better stories. It isn't fair!

The U.S. Supreme Court ruled in 1978 that women reporters

Mary Joe Fernandez finished high school before becoming a tennis pro. She is among the top players on the women's professional tennis circuit.

Manon Rheaume broke into professional hockey in 1992 with the Atlanta Knights, a minor league team in the Tampa Bay Lightning organization.

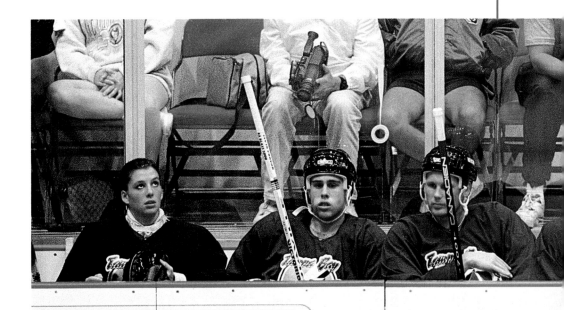

must be allowed in locker rooms if men reporters were, but the subject was still controversial more than 12 years later. In 1990 *Boston Herald* sports reporter Lisa Olson was harassed and verbally assaulted when she tried to conduct a postgame interview in the New England Patriots' locker room after a National Football League game.

BLAZING A TRAIL

Women are making advances in professional sports. Manon Rheaume is the first woman to play in a National Hockey League game. While a full-time goalie for the Atlanta Knights, one of the Tampa Bay Lightning's farm teams, Rheaume said she wasn't concerned with being a symbol for women. "I don't do this to be first," she once said. "I do it because I love hockey and because I have a chance." Knights' President Richard Adler said simply, "She's good for hockey."[11]

Rheaume is still a professional hockey player, a full-time goalie, in the minor leagues. Because of her, maybe more women will have the opportunity to play on professional hockey teams. "A lot of women talk to me," Rheaume once said. "They tell me, 'It's good what you do.' But that means nothing to me. I don't realize all the stuff I might mean to them."

Lyn St. James began drag racing when she was a teenager. An auto enthusiast, she liked to hang out with boys and work on cars. She

Lyn St. James, above, who finished 11th in the 1992 Indianapolis 500, followed in the footsteps of Janet Guthrie. Guthrie was the first woman in the famous auto race. She competed in the 1977 Indy 500.

won her first race at 17, but when she got older she decided to give up racing and become a secretary because she "never thought of [herself] as a race car driver."[12]

But try as she might to be "respectable," St. James couldn't stay away from racing for long. When her first husband encouraged her to take up driving again, she did, and eventually she became a professional.

Racing is "quite addictive," she once said.[16] St. James won the backing of the Ford Motor Company and J.C. Penney—she was the first woman to earn such important endorsements—and in 1992 she competed in the Indianapolis 500. She finished in 11th place. She is only the second woman ever to qualify for the prestigious race, and her fellow racers voted her Rookie of the Year.

St. James's skill and determination have impressed the men against whom she races. They praise her professionalism and driving ability. "She's a very smooth, natural driver," said Dick Simon, who owns the car that St. James drove in the 1993 Indy. "Do you see a woman competing with men in any other sport? No. And here she is competing against the best drivers in the world."[13]

PAM POSTEMA

When Pam Postema was a girl, she collected baseball cards. "By the time I was in fifth grade, I was hooked on sports," she said. "My sister had dried corsages and doily things pinned to her bulletin board. I had baseball and football pennants and photos of some of my favorite players."

Pam loved sports of all kinds, not just the sports girls were supposed to like. When she was six years old, she asked her parents to give her a kid-sized football uniform for Christmas. They did, and Pam was happy. "With sports, you knew where you stood," she said. "It didn't matter . . . if you were a girl or a boy."

After she graduated from high school, Pam wanted to find a job where she could use her athletic skill and ability. Her mother, knowing Pam's interest in baseball, suggested she become an umpire. Pam found a professional umpire school in Florida, and she signed up.

Umpire school was tough. The year was 1977, and Pam was one of the first two women accepted to the school. She had to prove herself to the male students and teachers.

After graduation, Pam was offered a job in a minor league in Florida. She accepted, and began a landmark 13-year career that ended in disappointment. Pam was one of

the first women to umpire in professional baseball. Some fans and
coaches didn't like the idea of a
woman doing what they considered
a man's job. They yelled at her from
the bleachers, and they argued her
decisions. Once, when she was umpiring a game in Colombia, South
America, an angry fan sent a death
threat to baseball officials. He said
he wanted to kill Pam!

Pam never stopped dreaming.
She wanted to umpire in the major
leagues, and for a time it looked as
if she might get that chance. Pam
worked hard, and slowly she made
her way to Class AAA baseball, the
minor leagues' top division. The next
step was the majors, and Pam was
ready. "I loved my job," she once
said. "I had my heart set on becoming a major league umpire."

But professional baseball struck
out Pam. In November 1989, the Of-
fice for Umpire Development in-
formed her that she had spent the
maximum number of years allowed
in the minor leagues, and she would
not be promoted to the majors. Pam
could no longer be a professional
umpire. She was fired.

Pam was angry. She was let go,
she said, because of her gender.
"Baseball wasn't ready for a woman
umpire no matter how good she

was," she said. Not everybody
agrees with Pam. Martin Springstead,
the American League's supervisor of
umpires, said every year many minor
league umpires compete for the few
open spots in the pros. Just 60
major league umpiring jobs are
available, he points out. It's diffi-
cult for anyone to become a major
league umpire.

Pam wrote in her autobiography
that she hopes that one day she can
be an umpire again. "Starting now,"
she wrote, "I'm determined to get
back into baseball and do it for
every . . . woman in the world."

Sources: Pam Postema, *You've Got To Have
Balls To Make It In This League, My Life as an
Umpire,* and Susan Reed and Lyndon Stambler, "The Umpire Strikes Back," *People,* May
25, 1992.

CHAPTER FIVE

WHAT'S AHEAD

■

In the last 20 years, women's participation in sports has grown by record numbers. Look back even further, and you discover that women and girls really have come a long way. But what changes does the future hold? What new and exciting advances lie ahead for women in sports? Will there be fewer "boys'" sports and "girls'" sports and more coed sports? Or will girls' sports opportunities continue to follow in the model of boys' sports, with more and more opportunities for elite athletes and fewer chances for average or more versatile athletes?

Jenny Hanley grew up playing ice hockey after Title IX. But since there weren't many girls' hockey teams, she played with boys most of the time. Hanley played youth hockey in her suburban community until high school, where she became the first girl goaltender on her school's hockey team.[1]

When Hanley went to college at Hamline University in Minnesota, she made national news. She tried out for the college hockey team, and was accepted as a first-string goaltender. She was the first woman to play on the team in her school's history.

While cracking the formerly all-boys' sport of ice hockey, goaltender Jenny Hanley found support from her teammates, but not always from opponents.

Later, Hanley transferred to the University of St. Thomas (also in Minnesota), and she played hockey there as well. Her playing skills were equal to or better than her male teammates', and she has earned the respect of coaches and fans. Still, Hanley says sometimes people make fun of her, or harass her when she's on the ice. "At any level, that shouldn't be accepted," she has told reporters. "It's common sense. You don't go to work and look at the secretary or any female you're working with and say vulgar things to her. Why should hockey be different?"[2]

Julie Croteau played on the St. Mary's College (Maryland) baseball team for three years before quitting because some of her own teammates taunted and harassed her. Still, Croteau says she thinks coed sports are a good idea because they give boys and girls a chance to know and respect each other as athletes. And she's an assistant coach for the Western New England College baseball team.[3] Meanwhile, Ila Borders became the first female athlete to pitch for a college baseball team. "College has definitely been hard to adjust to," said Borders, who attends Southern California College on a baseball scholarship. "Everybody

tells me I don't belong out here. Sometimes it gets to me, but no one's going to run me off."[4]

Because athletes like Hanley, Croteau, and Borders were willing to play on all-boys' teams, opportunities have opened for other girl athletes. In the future, Hanley predicts, other girls and young women will play on boys' and men's teams, just as she does. Maybe one day, women athletes will be a common sight in professional sports leagues.

Terry Abram, a former hockey coach and current high school administrator, says he finds the trend of women and men playing sports together encouraging. He said he'd like to see more women playing on men's professional teams. "I would love to see it," he said. "I definitely think it would add to the game."

Indeed, some women have played on men's professional teams, such as Lynette Woodard of the Harlem Globetrotters, and Nancy Lieberman-Cline of the now-defunct United States Basketball League as well as the Washington Senators (the Globetrotters' perpetual opponent).

Before she became a Harlem Globetrotter, Woodard was well-respected but not well-known as a basketball player. A standout in college, Woodard was playing on a women's professional team in Italy when she came back to the United States to play for the Globetrotters. During her two-year stint with the team, Woodard's salary was higher than any other American female playing professional basketball. She has often said that playing with men earned her the respect of people who'd never thought a woman could play basketball. "I helped change a lot of minds," she has said.[5] After Woodard's performance, in fact, Ann Meyers had a tryout with the Indiana Pacers of the National Basketball Association. Meyers didn't make the cut.

Manon Rheaume, the first female player in the National Hockey League, got her start playing with boys also. In her native Canada, she was one of the few girls in the Quebec Major Junior Hockey League. Rheaume was scouted for the major leagues, her coach has said, not because she is an oddity whose uniqueness helps to sell tickets, but because she is a good player—as good as most of her teammates.

For her part, Rheaume tries to play her best each time she is on the ice. She has said she hopes

Lynette Woodard

her experience can inspire others. "If I didn't try, I wouldn't know what I can do," she once said. "If I can help other people to have an ambition, that's good."[6]

BEYOND BOYS

Other female athletes compete directly with men in non-team sports. Lyn St. James races her car against men and wins. Julie Krone is a jockey, the first woman to ride in the Belmont Stakes in New York. Both women depend on their teammate—be it a car or horse—to help them win, but there's more to being a champion than having the right equipment. It takes brains, determination, skill, and strength.

Krone says winning a horse race takes self-confidence and humility. She's been riding horses

Jockey Julie Krone survived a serious fall in August of 1993, two months after she won the Belmont Stakes. She returned to racing in 1994.

A NEW OLYMPIC SPORT

Sitting at the pond's edge, a young girl laced her skates tight and pushed off, her silver blades cutting lines into the smooth ice. It was a brisk, dark evening not so many years ago.

As she picked up speed, the girl rounded a turn, crossing one skate in front of the other. She headed back across the rink at top speed, using an imaginary hockey stick to push an imaginary puck into an imaginary goal. As she skidded to a stop, thousands of imaginary fans cheered.

Even though she thought it could never happen in her lifetime, the girl pretended she was an Olympic hockey champion. In her mind's eye, she saw the stadium and the red, white, and blue uniforms. She even saw the three-level stand where the winning teams would hold their medals.

Lynn Olson, director of USA Hockey's girls' and women's program, said she could have been that girl on the ice. She loved to skate, and she loves to play hockey. She never dreamt that someday women's hockey would become an Olympic sport.

"My sisters and I skated when we were young, but girls couldn't play hockey then," Olson said. "We were avid sports enthusiasts, but there was nothing for us to compete in, except a marching unit. We all joined just to have something to do." Still, Olson never gave up on her dream. As she got older, she continued playing sports, especially winter ones. When she was 29, Olson was invited to join an all-women's hockey league. She jumped at the opportunity!

Lynn Olson

"I fell in love with the speed and finesse of the sport," Olson said. She decided more women and girls should be able to play hockey. Olson started hosting hockey camps and forming girls' hockey teams. "Hockey is such a wonderful sport," she said. "It shouldn't be just for boys."

Lots of people agreed with Olson. Girls went to the training camps and attended games. They signed up to play on teams. By 1993, there were 39 girls' teams in Olson's state, Minnesota, and many other girls played on boys' high school and college teams.

But Olson wasn't satisfied yet. Hockey is traditionally a men's game, and no women were on the board of directors at USA Hockey, the amateur sport's governing body. When a seat came open, Olson ran for it. She was elected in 1989. Since then, she's pushed for equal treatment and funding for girls' teams. Olson is proudest of the fact that the Olympic committee approved women's hockey as an official sport, starting with the 1998 Winter Games.

"It's a real victory for women's sports," Olson said of the Olympic designation. "To be recognized internationally, to be taken seriously enough to compete in the Olympics, for me, that's a dream come true."

Source: Interview with Lynn Olson.

Julie Krone says competing against men isn't the issue. She thinks competing against oneself, trying always to do better, is the real challenge.

in contests since she was five years old, winning in a sport that is dominated by males. "You have to be a confident person," Krone has said. "And when you're doing well, you have to stay humble, although you might be flying in the clouds and feeling so happy you can't stand it."[7]

Krone's professional attitude and skill helps her win lots of prize money. She is considered one of the top jockeys in the world, taking home more than $30 million in 10 seasons. But, Krone says, success hasn't come easily. "Even if you keep getting slapped down, you have to keep going back and trying," she once said. "You have to have this unconditional dedication."[8]

Many sports experts feel that playing side-by-side with men or competing against men in non-team sports is one way female athletes can earn the respect and attention they deserve. Others say women-versus-women events will become more popular, drawing larger crowds and bigger sponsors.

Terry Abram said girl athletes could only benefit if women's sports got the same kind of attention as men's. "It would help them feel that their contributions were just as important," he said. "Now girls have very few role models in professional sports."

BY LEAPS AND BOUNDS

Some sports researchers maintain that women's times in certain endurance events—including long-distance swimming and marathon running—will one day surpass men's. Women already have beaten men in international dogsledding events—a sport that requires endurance, patience, and

skill with animals. And women have won swimming contests and ultra-marathons (races of extra-long distance).

Women's times in long-distance races are dropping rapidly when compared with men's. An example is the women's 1,500-meter race, which was added to the Olympics in 1972. The women's world record dropped from 4:01:04 that year to 3:52:47 in 1980. The men's world record in that same period went from 3:33:1 to 3:30:77.

INCREDIBLE BULKS

Lenda Murray can pick up a 315-pound barbell and hoist it over her head. When she flexes her muscles, people turn and stare; her huge biceps pop and ripple, and her legs bulge like iron beams.

Murray is Ms. Olympia 1993, the best female bodybuilder in the world. With muscles bigger than most men's, she's used to people staring, but she doesn't care. She's won the Ms. Olympia contest every year since 1990. "Sometimes I think I scare people," she has said.

Less than 20 years ago, when women first started entering bodybuilding contests, women with big muscles were considered strange. Nowadays, even though people still stare at female bodybuilders, many are staring in envy rather than in fright. "Suddenly it's OK for a woman to look strong," said one female bodybuilding champion in Chicago. "Suddenly bodybuilding is no longer just for men."

Men have been building their bodies for centuries, but weightlifting didn't really catch on as a sport until the 1950s. In the 1960s and 1970s, hoards of gigantic men flocked to Muscle Beach, California, to lift heavy barbells on the sand under the hot sun. They pumped iron for hours, building bigger and bigger muscles in their search for the perfect physique. Some even took dangerous illegal drugs, called anabolic steroids, to make their muscles bigger.

Women's bodybuilding became popular in the late 1970s. The first contests were little more than beauty pageants, with too-thin women posing in bikinis and high heels. "The judges preferred it that way," the Chicago lifter said. "They didn't want women to look too much like men. It was ridiculous."

Things have changed. While past contests emphasized "femininity" and "grace," modern women bodybuilders are judged for muscle development and strength. And the winners are getting more and more muscular.

Bev Francis deserves credit for changing the face of women's bodybuilding. An Australian native with muscles of gargantuan proportions, Francis sent the judges into a tailspin when she entered the Caesar's Cup competition in 1983. No one had ever seen a woman with muscles so big.

Francis placed eighth in the competition, but women's bodybuilding has never been the same. She challenged traditional ideas about feminine beauty, and she went on to win the Ms. Olympia title in 1987.

Other champions have followed Francis's lead, piling on bigger and

Lenda Murray

bigger layers of muscles and abandoning high heels and dance routines for bare feet and eye-popping poses. Lenda Murray is no exception. She's proud of her muscles and the dedication it took to build them, and she sees a future when other women will be, too.

That future in mind, when ordinary people are taken aback by her appearance, Murray just smiles.

"People sometimes don't know what to say when they see me," she once said. "They say something like 'You're so big.' I just say 'Thank you.'"

Sources: Nick Ravo, "Wonder Woman, in the Flesh," *New York Times,* December 2, 1992, and Mariah Burton Nelson, *Are We Winning Yet? How Women Are Changing Sports and Sports Are Changing Women* (Random House: New York, 1991).

Women such as Paula Newby-Fraser, a regular winner of triathlons, have expanded the expectations of women in sports. Triathlons are grueling competitions that involve a 2.4-mile swim, an 112-mile bike race, and a 26.2-mile run.

In her book *The Woman Runner,* author Gloria Averbuch writes: "Comparisons are made showing dramatic gains for women versus men at all distances. In fact, the average life span of a world record for men is 5.3 years, while for women it is 2.2 years. The performance gap is only 10 percent and closing, and some experts predict equal performances at all distances by men and women in 20 to 30 years."[9]

Whether male and female athletes ever achieve equality on the courts, fields, and diamonds of sports might not even be worth recording. Perhaps with the inclusion of female athletes into the sports world, the individual accomplishments of all athletes can be appreciated, regardless of their race, sex, or sport.

"I see a trend toward more respect for the accomplishments of women," said Dorothy McIntyre, assistant executive director of the Minnesota State High School League, "but in order to continue to educate the public, we still need another generation of women to pass through that full athletic experience. We need women who understand the benefits and importance of athletics to come of age and take part in

Endurance events, such as triathlons and sled dog races, have provided men and women with opportunities to compete against one another. Libby Riddles, a musher who won the prestigious Iditarod dogsled race in 1985, is evidence that training, dedication, and talent are often more important than gender.

leadership, in teaching others to respect the achievements of women athletes."

Great women athletes like Jackie Joyner-Kersee help break down stereotypes, according to McIntyre. Joyner-Kersee's athletic

Jackie Joyner-Kersee won Olympic gold medals in the heptathlon in 1988 and 1992. Joyner-Kersee is a role model for all athletes—men and women.

achievements have inspired some sportswriters to call her "The Athlete of the Century." She is so good that her gender becomes less important than her athletic achievements.

"This is something I hope to see continue indefinitely," McIntyre said. "Maybe someday athletes will just be athletes, not women, men, boys, or girls. Maybe someday athletes will be judged by their abilities, and not their gender."

NOTES

CHAPTER 1: GETTING IN THE GAME

1. Allen Guttmann, *Women's Sports: A History* (New York: Columbia University Press, 1991), p. 215.

2. Lynn Jaffee and Rebecca Manzer, "Girls' Perspectives: Physical Activity and Self-Esteem," *Melpomene Journal,* Autumn 1992, pp. 14-23.

3. *Gender Equity and Athletics: A Manual to Assist Minnesota High Schools to Conduct a Self-Review of their Athletic Programs.* Minnesota State High School League. January 1993.

4. Adrianne Blue, *Grace Under Pressure, The Emergence of Women in Sport* (London: Sodgwick & Jackson, 1987), pp. 60-61.

5. Gloria Averbuch, *The Woman Runner: Free to be the Complete Athlete* (New York: Simon and Schuster, 1984), pp. 5-6.

6. Mariah Burton Nelson, *Are We Winning Yet? How Women are Changing Sports and Sports are Changing Women* (New York: Random House, 1991), p. 87.

CHAPTER 2: BEING A WINNER

1. Lynn Jaffee and Rebecca Manzer, "Girls' Perspectives: Physical Activity and Self-Esteem," *Melpomene Journal,* Autumn 1992, pp. 14-23.

2. Carol Gilligan, *A Different Voice* (Cambridge, Mass.: Harvard University Press, 1982).

3. Kay Porter and Judy Foster, *The Mental Athlete, Inner Training for Peak Performance* (New York: Ballantine Books, 1987), pp. 128-130.

4. Mariah Burton Nelson, *Are We Winning Yet? How Women are Changing Sports and Sports are Changing Women* (New York: Random House, 1991), p. 87.

5. *The Women's Sports Foundation Report: Minorities in Sports: The Effect of Varsity Sports Participation on the Social, Educational, and Career Mobility of Minority Students.* Women's Sports Foundation. 1989.

6. Tom Biracree, *Althea Gibson: Tennis Champion* (New York: Chelsea House Publishers, 1989).

7. Mary A. Boutilier and Lucinda SanGiovanni, *The Sporting Woman* (Champaign, Ill.: Human Kinetics, 1983), pp. 98-99.

CHAPTER 3: OFF THE SIDELINES

1. Matthew Goodman, "Little League Justice," *Utne Reader,* September/October 1990, pp. 118-119.

2. *Gender Equity and Athletics: A Manual to Assist Minnesota High Schools to Conduct a Self-Review of their Athletic Programs.* Minnesota State High School League. January 1993.

3. Allen Guttmann, *Women's Sports: A History* (New York: Columbia University Press, 1991), p. 215.

4. The American Association of University Women, "How Schools Shortchange Girls," 1992, pp. 45-46.

5. R. Vivian Acosta and Linda Jean Carpenter, *Women in Intercollegiate Sport: A Longitudinal Study—Fifteen Year Update 1977-1992.* Unpublished manuscript, Brooklyn College, Brooklyn, New York, 1992.

6. Andrea Steiner, "Park Plan Targets Girls' Self-Image," *Minnesota Women's Press,* 27 March 1991.

7. National Collegiate Athletic Association, *Survey of NCAA Member Institutions on the Elimination and Addition of Sports,* Mission, Kansas, 1988.

8. Mary Jordan, "Only One School Meets Gender Equity Goal," *Washington Post,* 21 June 1992, p. D1.

9. Ed Sherman, "Gender Equity," *Chicago Tribune* series in *St. Paul Pioneer Press,* 10-14 May 1993.

10. Sherman, "Gender Equity."

11. Jay Weiner, "Making (her)story," *Minneapolis Star Tribune,* 24 January 1993, p. 1C.

12. "Fundamentals Apply in Education," *NCAA News,* 19 August 1992, p. 4.

13. Margaret Carlisle Duncan, "Sports Photographs and Sexual Difference: Images of Women and Men in the 1984 and 1988 Olympic Games," *Sociology of Sport Journal 7,* 1990, pp. 22-43.

CHAPTER 4: PRO DREAMS

1. Harry Edwards, *Sociology of Sport* (Homewood, Ill.: The Dorsey Press, 1973), p. 273.

2. Lisa Dillman, "Life After College," *The Sporting News,* 13 April 1992, p. 20.

3. Dave Kindred, "A Different Dream," *The Sporting News,* 10 August 1992, p. 18.

4. Kindred, "A Different Dream."

5. Curry Kirkpatrick, "Not Just a Dream," *Sports Illustrated,* 8 June 1992, p. 41.

6. Jerry Kirshenbaum, "Yanks in Japan," *Sports Illustrated,* 8 February 1993, p. 9

7. Martina Navratilova, *Martina* (New York: Alfred A. Knopf, Inc., 1985), p. 268.

8. Allen Guttmann, *Women's Sports: A History* (New York: Columbia University Press), pp. 209-210.

9. Sally Jenkins, "Racket Science," *Sports Illustrated,* 29 April 1991, pp. 66-78.

10. Jenkins, "Racket Science."

11. Jay Weiner, "Making (her)story," *Minneapolis Star Tribune,* 24 January 1993, p. 1C.

12. William Plummer, "Speed Queen," *People,* 31 May 1993, pp. 83-84.

13. Plummer, "Speed Queen."

CHAPTER 5: WHAT'S AHEAD?

1. Jay Weiner, "Hanley Finds Niche in Nets with Tommies," *Minneapolis Star Tribune,* 24 January 1993, p. 8C.

2. Weiner, "Hanley Finds Niche."

3. Mariah Burton Nelson, *The Stronger Women Get, The More Men Love Football, Sexism and the American Culture of Sports* (New York: Harcourt Brace and Company, 1994), pp. 83, 100.

4. Shelley Smith, "Sports People," *Sports Illustrated,* 7 March 1994, pp. 66-67.

5. Matthew Newman, *Lynette Woodard* (Minnesota: Crestwood House, 1986).

6. Jay Weiner, "Making (her)story," *Minneapolis Star Tribune,* 24 January 1993, p. 1C.

7. Susan R. Dillon, "Jockeying for the Top," *Women's Sports and Fitness,* November/December 1991, pp. 64-65.

8. Dillon, "Jockeying for the Top."

9. Gloria Averbuch, *The Woman Runner, Free to be the Complete Athlete* (New York: Simon and Schuster, 1984), p. 168.

BIBLIOGRAPHY

INTERVIEWS WITH AUTHOR

Jaffee, Lynn, Program Coordinator, Melpomene Institute. December 1992.

Kane, Mary Jo, Sports Sociologist, University of Minnesota, School of Kinesiology and Leisure Arts. February 1993.

Kordonowy, Janet, Former Girls' Athletic Association participant. December 1992.

McIntyre, Dorothy, Assistant Executive Director, Minnesota State High School League. February 1993.

Minkinen, Andrea, St. Paul (Minnesota) firefighter. February 1993.

Olson, Lynn, Director of USA Hockey's Girls'/Women's Division. December 1992 and February 1993.

Owen, Kelley, Hockey coach and player. December 1992.

Reith, Kathryn, Communications Director, Women's Sports Foundation. February 1993.

Tongen, Jennifer, Former Girls' Athletic Association participant. December 1992.

Voelz, Chris, Athletic Director, University of Minnesota Women's Intercollegiate Athletic Department. February 1993.

BOOKS, MAGAZINES, NEWSPAPERS, AND UNPUBLISHED MANUSCRIPTS

Acosta, Vivian and Linda Jean Carpenter. *Women in Intercollegiate Sport: A Longitudinal Study—Fifteen Year Update 1977-1992.* Unpublished manuscript, Brooklyn College, Brooklyn, New York, 1992.

American Association of University Women. *Shortchanging Girls, Shortchanging America,* 1991.

Athletic Footwear Association. *Fit to Achieve,* 1991.

Attner, Paul. "The Ultimate Athlete." *The Sporting News,* 10 August 1992.

Averbuch, Gloria. *The Woman Runner: Free to be the Complete Athlete.* Simon and Schuster: New York, 1984.

Biracree, Tom. *Althea Gibson, Tennis Champion.* Chelsea House Publishers: New York, 1989.

Blue, Adrianne. *Grace Under Pressure, The Emergence of Women in Sport.* London: Sodgwick & Jackson, 1987.

Boutilier, Mary A. and Lucinda SanGiovanni. *The Sporting Woman.* Human Kinetics: Illinois, 1983.

Bruning, Fred. "Into the Den of the Dinosaur." *Maclean's,* 22 October 1990.

Chrysler Fund-AAU Physical Fitness Program. *Physical Fitness Trends in American Youth: A Ten-Year Study, 1980-1990.* 1989.

Dillman, Lisa. "Life After College." *The Sporting News,* 13 April 1992.

Dillon, Susan R. "Jockeying for the Top." *Women's Sports and Fitness,* November/December 1991.

Duncan, Margaret Carlisle. "Sports Photographs and Sexual Difference: Images of Women and Men in the 1984 and 1988 Olympic Games." *Sociology of Sport Journal 7,* 1990.

"Fundamentals Apply in Education." *NCAA News.* 19 August 1992.

Gilligan, Carol. *A Different Voice.* Cambridge, Mass.: Harvard University Press, 1982.

Goodman, Matthew. "Little League Justice." *Utne Reader,* September/October 1990.

"Great Olympic Moments: Jackie Joyner-Kersee Seoul 1988." *Ebony,* April 1992.

Guttmann, Allen. *Women's Sports: A History.* Columbia University Press: New York, 1991.

Herwig, Carol. "Many Women Fear Stalling on Title IX." *USA Today,* 8 June 1992.

Jaffee, Lynn and Rebecca Manzer. "Girls' Perspectives: Physical Activity and Self-Esteem." *Melpomene Journal,* Autumn 1992.

Jenkins, Sally. "Racket Science." *Sports Illustrated,* 29 April 1991.

Johnson, Earvin and William Novak. *My Life.* Random House: New York, 1992.

Jordan, Mary. "Only One School Meets Gender Equity Goal." *Washington Post,* 21 June 1992.

Kindred, Dave. "A Different Dream." *The Sporting News,* 10 August 1992.

King, Billie Jean with Frank Deford. *Billie Jean.* Viking Press: New York, 1982.

Kirkpatrick, Curry. "Not Just a Dream." *Sports Illustrated,* 8 June 1992.

Kirshenbaum, Jerry. "A Law that Needs New Muscle." *Sports Illustrated,* 4 March 1985.

Kirshenbaum, Jerry. "Yanks in Japan." *Sports Illustrated,* 8 February 1993.

Knudson, R. R. *Babe Didrikson: Athlete of the Century.* Viking Kestrel: New York, 1985.

Lee, Mabel. *A History of Physical Education and Sports in the U.S.A.* New York: John Wiley and Sons, 1983.

Lieber, Jill. "Going for Three." *Sports Illustrated,* 8 February 1993.

Lieberman-Cline, Nancy with Debby Jennings. *Lady Magic: The Autobiography of Nancy Lieberman-Cline.* Champaign, Ill.: Sagamore Publishing, Inc., 1992.

Minnesota State High School League. *Gender Equity and Athletics.* January 1993.

Monaghan, George. "Female Athletes in 2nd Place." *Star Tribune,* 16 June 1992.

National Collegiate Athletic Association. *Survey of NCAA Member Institutions on the Elimination and Addition of Sports.* Mission, Kansas, 1988.

Navratilova, Martina, with George Vecsey. *Martina.* New York: Alfred A. Knopf, Inc., 1985.

Nelson, Mariah Burton. *Are We Winning Yet? How Women Are Changing Sports and Sports Are Changing Women.* Random House: New York, 1991.

Nelson, Mariah Burton. *The Stronger Women Get, The More Men Love Football, Sexism and the American Culture of Sports.* New York: Harcourt Brace and Company, 1994.

Newman, Matthew. *Lynette Woodard.* Crestwood House: Minnesota, 1986.

Pavicic, Barbara J. "Women Athletes Trivialized by Media Images." *Minnesota Women's Press,* 27 March 1991.

Plummer, William. "Speed Queen." *People,* 31 May 1993.

Plummer, William. "Woman Among Wildcats." *People,* 22 March 1993.

Porter, Kay, and Judy Foster. *The Mental Athlete: Inner Training for Peak Performance.* New York: Ballantine Books, 1987.

Postema, Pam and Gene Wojciechowski. *You've Got to Have Balls to Make it in this League: My Life as an Umpire.* (New York: Simon and Schuster, 1992).

Ravo, Nick. "Wonder Woman, in the Flesh." *New York Times,* 2 December 1992.

Reed, Susan, and Lyndon Stambler. "The Umpire Strikes Back." *People,* 25 May 1992.

Sherman, Ed. "Gender Equity." Series in *St. Paul Pioneer Press,* 10-14 May 1993.

Smith, Karen M. "Title IX and Gender Equity." University of Minnesota-Twin Cities Women's Intercollegiate Athletics, November 1992.

Smith, Shelley. "Sports People," *Sports Illustrated,* 7 March 1994.

Sparhawk, Ruth M. (et. al.) *American Women in Sport, 1887-1987: A 100-year Chronology.* The Scarecrow Press: New Jersey, 1989.

Stanek, Carolyn. *The Complete Guide to Women's College Athletics.* Contemporary Books: Chicago, 1981.

Steiner, Andrea. "Park Plan Targets Girls' Self-Image." *Minnesota Women's Press,* 27 March 1991.

Steiner, Andy. "Iron Butterflies." *The Monitor,* 1992.

Sullivan, George. *Great Lives: Sports.* Charles Scribner's Sons: New York, 1988.

Taylor, Phil. "Music City Madness." *Sports Illustrated,* 8 February 1983.

Weiner, Jay. "Giving it the Old College Try Can be Tough." *Star Tribune,* 24 January 1993.

Weiner, Jay. "Hanley Finds Niche in Nets with Tommies." *Star Tribune,* 24 January 1993.

Weiner, Jay. "Making (her)story: Finally, Females Getting their Shot at Hockey as Rheaume Leads the Way." *Star Tribune,* 24 January 1993.

Wilson Sporting Goods Company and the Women's Sports Foundation. *The Wilson Report: Moms, Dads, Daughters, and Sports.* November-December, 1987.

Women's Sports Foundation. *The Women's Sports Foundation Report: Minorities in Sports: The Effect of Varsity Sports Participation on the Social, Educational, and Career Mobility of Minority Students.* 1989.

INDEX

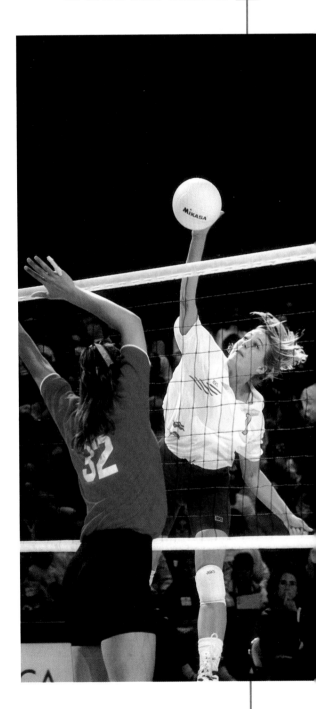

ACKNOWLEDGMENTS

Photographs are reproduced with the permission of: pp. 2, 66, Jim Gund/ALLSPORT; pp. 6, 78, Nancie Battaglia/USA Hockey; pp. 8, 21, John Ferko/Swarthmore College; p. 9, Melpomene Institute; p. 10, Jean Higgins/Unicorn Stock Photos; p. 11, MPLIC; pp. 13, 17, 31, 32, 36, 53, 70, 71, UPI/Bettmann; p. 14, Chris Boylan/Unicorn Stock Photos; p. 15, University of Minnesota, Intramural Program; pp. 19, 23, © Mickey Pfleger; p. 20, Minnesota Amateur Sports Commission; p. 30, Olympic Festival/ Minnesota Amateur Sports Commission; p. 24, Phillip C. Roullard; p. 25, John Biever; pp. 26, 81, 96, Macalester College; pp. 27, 40, 41, 50, 93, Gerry Vuchetich/University of Minnesota Women's Athletics; p. 28, International Tennis Hall of Fame and Tennis Museum at The Newport Casino, Newport, Rhode Island; p. 34, 67, Scott Halleran/ ALLSPORT; p. 37, SportsChrome East/West, Robert Tringali Jr.; p. 38, Minnesota Amateur Sports Commission/Michael J. Prokosch; p. 39, Tom McCarthy/ Unicorn Stock Photos; p. 43, © 1993 Jim Brown; p. 44, Clive Brunskill/ALLSPORT; p. 45, Ken Levine/ALLSPORT; p. 46, The University of Nebraska, Lincoln; p. 47, University of Iowa, Women's Athletic Department; p. 49, University of Kentucky; pp. 51, 59, Tony Duffy/ALLSPORT; p. 55, Chris Cole/ALLSPORT; p. 57, Northern Indiana Historical Society; p. 58, Aneal Vohra/Unicorn Stock Photos; p. 60, Sharon Hoogstraten/ TEAMTENNIS; p. 61, © Carol L. Newsom; pp. 62, 76, Harlem Globetrotters; p. 65, Gary M. Prior/ALLSPORT; pp. 68, 69, Steve Swope/ALLSPORT; p. 72, Minnesota Amateur Sports Commission/Phil Stephens Photography; p. 74, University of St. Thomas, Instructional Support Services; p. 77, Shaun Botterill/ALLSPORT; p. 79, USA Hockey; p. 80, SportsChrome East/West; p. 83, Bill Dobbins/ALLSPORT; p. 84, C.J. Olivares Jr./ALLSPORT; p. 85, John S. Foster; p. 86, SportsChrome East/West, Louis A. Raynor.

Cover photograph by Jim Commetucci/ALLSPORT.